I'M 25

25 Poems, Songs, and Deep Thoughts of Orangesticity

Leslie Guity

BK
ROYSTON
Publishing

BK Royston Publishing
P. O. Box 4321
Jeffersonville, IN 47131
502-802-5385
http://www.bkroystonpublishing.com
bkroystonpublishing@gmail.com

Cover Design: Leslie Guity

Cover Layout: Elite Covers

ISBN-13: 978-1-951941-56-7

Printed in the United States of America

Dedication

I have been going through some interesting times and God sent angels to watch over and help me through.

I love my family — I love each and every one of them, but I have to dedicate this book to my mom, my Dona, who checks on you every single morning to make sure you are well.

I would also like to shout out my sister Tania Guity and my niece Ceecee (Talia). Kudos to you on your first book.

They are always there to remind me of who I am and to keep moving forward.

I would like to shout out to Gina Fernandes and Leelee, my sista sista. She literally helped me clean my house both physically and spiritually. Love you forever.

Continue to rest in paradise Ms. Linda Johnson, my earth angel and street mom.

Table of Contents

Preface

I titled the book "I'm **25**" because whenever someone asks my age, I say I'm **25**. In fact, I have been telling people that for the past two decades.

I say it so much that when I state my real age, I startle myself.

I have an 8-year-old niece, Talia, whom I call Ceecee and she calls me Ceecee. She is a fellow new author.

 She is quick to remind me how old I really am.

One day she said to me, "You know you in your fiddies."

The number **25** is a significant number in my life. I was born on the **25**th day of the month.

My favorite number is 7. 2 + 5 = 7.

These are the reasons I hand-picked **25** poems, songs, and deep thoughts to share out of my collection of poetry, which I have been writing throughout the years.

Oh And Orangesticity, You ask what that is?

I have always loved the color orange. I have for the better part of my life, so I made up the word orangesticity, which is orange, majestic, and city put together.

Clever, huh? I made this word and the word "orangestic 1" when I was 15 and it stuck with me.

Well, I have to go now. Please enjoy the works that have been living in my heart.

1. God Breathed 7/27/2019

2 Timothy 3:16–17 inspired this poem

I do not write my own works.
I just hold the pen in my hand and wait…
I look down in my heart for the words,
Searching for one word… 6, 7, then 8.

I desire God to be glorified.
I desire God to be pleased.
Therefore, I am glad to say
That all my works are God breathed.

The pen is stroked with every breath.
It comes from deep within my soul.
I listen for direction, and green light does
mean go.

Writing poems of building, of correction, of
love,
Yes. They all come from the breath sent
from up above.

God breathed in me,
So, I breathe in the through my nose and out
through my mouth.
Breathing in joy and peace and
Breathing out fear and doubt.

So glad that God uses me to inspire, to
share, to bring peace.
Blessed that all my works come because in
me God breathed.

2. God Is Working It Out

God is working it out, working it out, working it out, working it out, working it out, working it out for my good.

For He is working it out, working it out, working it out for my good.

Behind the scenes, He is making it clean and ironing the wrinkles.

You've been redeemed

A delightful place

Run your race

Pain and suffering

You're in the right space.

3. God Makes Beautiful Things 2/16/2016

He made the flowers and the trees and birds on them to sing.

He made the sunrise and sunset.

He made the mountains and the sea,

The high points and depth,

Valleys and canyons,

Deserts so hot.

He made everything so beautifully, better than the biggest diamond ever bought.

He made the butterflies and the bees,

The bayou so peaceful.

Everything that He touched, He made it so beautiful.

He had Jesus to die on the cross for our sin.

Victories we win

When we invite God in.

And God made you and me in love, with talents and gifts so unique on purpose.

And we are

Beautiful.

4. A Tribute to Mi Madre

I'd like to present to you a beautiful woman
who birthed me.

She is loving, encouraging, and inspiring.

She is caring, giving, and smart.

So glad God made her to be mi madre.

Beauty exudes from her heart.

Thank you madre,

My Dona,

You are a blessing

And full of grace.

I love you with everything I got.

I will honor you 'til the end of my days.

Con todo mi Corazon.

5. Mothering 4/3/00

Being a mother is a blessing from God.

He's entrusting you with His children, the peas of a pod.

He teaches you how to discipline and show them His way.

They will make you proud when all your teachings are displayed.

So, take the mothering very seriously.

The children are our future and you take part in who they turn out to be.

Mothering is an art that God instills within us.

If you are a mother, you are an artist with a Godly paint brush.

6. God sends angels, I say
1/17/2020

God sends angels, I say

He sent me two when I moved around the way.

One was Ms. A and the other was Ms. L. J.

They greeted me when I first came on their block,

Making me feel at ease.

God sends angels, I say

Put there for anything I needed.

Raising five kids single handedly was not an easy task.

They cooked for me and the children without me having to ask.

The relationship between Ms. L.J. and me grew to the point where I now call her my street mom.

We shared a lot in common so closer became our bond.

We'd sit on the porch and talk sometimes until nightfall.

Her pot roast was so good I barely shared with the kids; I ate it all.

God sends angels, I say.

When Ma L.J. fell ill, harder did I pray.

Prayed for doctors and nurses that they would help her in any way.

Prayed for health and wholeness throughout her being.

Whatever God's will for her life was, that was yet to be seen.

Though I am a Hallmark viewer, Mom had me watching action movies.

Even when she was weak, she was trying to still help me.

Brought her an angel ornament to watch over her through her journey.

Little did I know that she was an earth angel sent by God for you and me.

Mom, the earth angel has returned to a higher post.

Hanging out with God and the heavenly host.

I gave an angel to an angel.

God sends angels I say,

My angel.

7. God Says, It Is Me You Are Looking For.... 6/14/2007

Why are you looking back?

Why are you looking left and right?

You should be looking up, what you need is right in your sight.

I know you have been hurt before

So, for others you have closed the door... to your heart....

God says I have to tell you something.

It is me you are looking for.

You were in a marriage that you thought would last.

You were having trouble forgetting everything in your past.

God is waiting for you to cast all your cares.

He will give you comfort and His love He will share... with you.

God says It is me you are looking for.

I pray for you to get to the place
where you stay in God's face.
I pray you would see God's way
I pray that you will hear God say
That it is me you are looking for.

8. A Love Lesson 7/10/2014

If you look back in time you can find

Someone who was checking on you all the time.

You thought they were bothering you,

Getting in your stuff.

You thought they were being annoying

And they talked too much.

But those were the people who really cared

The ones you should be listening to

And pull up a chair.

They were concerned that you were going

Down the wrong path.

And when you smelled and were dirty,

Sent you to take a bath.

We have to pay attention!

There are people who want to see you crack,

But make it seem that they have your back.

Some people that you think love you

Want to see you fail,

And nowhere around when you find yourself in jail,

Not even money in your canteen or a cigarette.

Cold shoulder is what you're going to get.

Not all people who say they love you really do.

You will really know their love when they show you.

Love is an action word.

See what you heard,

Pretending is absurd,

And for the birds.

Listen. Take heed!

Succeed. Agreed?

Discern who is friend and who is not.

Up in nonsense is where you will get caught.

If your best is what they want from you, they love you.

If asked to participate in negativity, get them away from you.

Life is too precious,

Too valuable, and too short.

There are people who genuinely love you,

Who pretend to,

And all other sorts.

Remember, there are the ones who want to see you progress,

And there are ones who will lead you into a negative mess.

Love promotes

And

Hate provokes.

You have a choice between a curse and a blessing.

Please study and learn this valuable love lesson.

9. Extra Sugar (Date Unknown)

I'm an extra sugar sista.

You know, the kind who is smiling and joying all the time.

The type whose laughter is like a bell chime.

Most times, in a good mood.

Sorta like when a man's belly is full

I'm an extra sugar sista

You know, the kind who cares for the children and on the PTA,

The type that listens to your problems and knows just what to say.

Most times puts others before herself in all that she does.

Sorta like butter I try to spread love.

Because I'm an extra sugar sista.

10. BIG 4/12/12

Yes, my lips are big, the better to kiss you with.

Yes, my breasts are big, the better to squeeze with.

Yes, my heart is big, the better to love you with.

The truth is someone can have big ears just to listen to you with.

And they can have big feet to carry you with.

And just be plain old BIG to reach something that you can't.

Big is not always a bad thing.

Big can be beautiful and a blessing, the better to bless you with.

BIG blessing, BIG lesson.

11. I see you 6/15–16/2009

I see you

How lovely you are

You don't think so

But you are beautiful

And that is something you need to know.

I see you

A little apprehensive

A little bit of self-doubt

You are a child of God

So, what's that all about?

I see you

A little jealousy

A little bit of pride

But God lives in you

And in you He shall abide.

I see you

Hurt and broken

Lack the art of forgiveness

Unless you let go

You won't find happiness.

I see you

Bad decisions

Looking for love

If you look up

Real love comes from above.

I see you

How lovely you are

But you don't think so

You sure are so beautiful

This is something you need to know.

I see you
Yet a caring one
Many gifts you hold
That God has given to you
Including riches untold.

I see you
Growing, blossoming, beautifully
No longer a bud but a flower
Made fearfully and wonderfully.

I see you
So lovely and beautiful
Made fearfully and wonderfully
I see you.

12. Use the Front Door 8/2004

Stop trying to come in through the back door.

The front door is open for you to come in if you choose.

In fact, the front door is what the kings use.

Are you a king or what?

What are you looking through the window for?

You are a child of God.

So, come in through the front door.

Back doors are for demons who steal and lie.

Ones who do their own thing and now their hearts cry.

Jesus says, "seek Him first and things will be given to you."

Stop trying the back door

When the front door is open to walk through.

Bet you feel you're worthless and don't deserve honor,

And that the back door is more suitable,

Because you are a goner.

Run up to the front door, all your burdens to Him you cast.

I'm telling you God has forgiven all the sins of your past.

You're are a king, you are rich.

You are not poor, so stop trying to come in through the back door.

Kings, Queens, use the front door.

13.   I AM A QUEEN!!!!
9/9/2008

I am A Queen! You know what I mean?

You think you can speak to me in that way

So it seems?

Well I think not 'cause I am blessed.

You think the way you act toward me

Will get me stressed?

You will not talk to me in that tone

I demand respect; your attitude I will not condone!

I am a Queen! I am as rich as can be.

I always get everything that I need,

For I belong to God; He is my Dad.

Stand when I come thru the door might I add.

Don't try to dis' me 'cause I'm not the one.

I have the victory and I've already won.

Not you or no devil will mess with me

'cause I will just stand very firm and you have to flee.

Trying to walk all over me, don't even go there.

You will surely pay the price; I'll just say a prayer.

I am a child of God, don't you agree?

Like royalty is the way you will acknowledge me.

I am a Queen! I am beautiful.

Baby, open your eyes.

I'm an heiress of God. You better recognize

That the Queen is: Me!

14. The Power, Your Purpose, Your Dreams 6/13/2014

The power is in you fulfilling your purpose, not behind a gun.

As a youth you should be getting education and just having fun.

Somewhere along the line we have lost our way.

Our paths are sent before us, each and every day.

We fail to see our importance and look at the purpose of someone else,

Thinking the grass is greener on the other side of the fence.

The power is not just in your friend, aunt, parent or teacher, too.

You have to look deeper because the power is inside of you.

Whatever you have a passion for, that's what it's all about.

That thing that's in your heart, go ahead just let it out.

If you wanna sing, sing. If you wanna dance, dance. If you invent, invent.

If you wanna rap, rap. Just do something you are really good at.

I know you have visions and I know you have dreams. God is the ice and you are the cream.

Dreams are like grass: if it's watered, it will grow fast, but if it is dry it will die and won't last.

With your joy, enjoy, enjoy, enjoy, and with your heartache create, create, create.

The pain you go through helps you write great songs.

Most times we are trying to fit in or trying to belong.

WE are meant to stand out, we are meant to shine.

Because we refuse to pursue our purpose, inside we are dying.

Therefore, some of us lose hope and we get angry; probably because we are running from who we are…

Supposed to be.

In not pushing toward your purpose, some of us are rude.

What we really need to do is check our attitudes.

We don't wanna work; we want everything handed to us.

We want everything now and can't just go through the process.

Flowers don't bloom in a day. Most prayers are not answered right away.

We think the ones who hate us, love us.

And that the evil doer is righteous.

WE cannot move forward if our thinking pattern is backwards.

When we say or hear something good, we say that's stupid.

When we like something, we say that it's PHAT.

Now what kind of thinking is that?

Saggin' pants, dagger dance, disrespect your mother, kill your brother.

Let's call things what they are...good is good and evil is evil.

Let's not get confused. Confusion is of the devil.

So what, you have fatherlessness and brokenness in your history.

When you fulfill your purpose, you will have a testimony.

Don't listen to haters, fulfill your destiny.

Let's determine to find/fulfill your purpose and follow our dreams,

And not to be someone else and not to envy.

You are at your weakest when you put your dreams on the shelf.

The most powerful you become is when you just be yourself.

15. I'm Having a Baby/The Birth of My Purpose
12/21/2007

One night I was intimate with God and a seed was planted deep.

My belly was then filled with songs, visions, poems and dreams.

I knew that I have conceived because I found myself craving

Cookies and ice cream.

As I started to grow in the first trimester,

I was told by God to prepare.

I hear Him tell me things to do,

Things that I wouldn't normally dare.

The songs stirred up in my spirit,

First the verse, then chorus and then the vamp.

Songs were coming so fast that I bent over with cramps.

Poems just a flowing and when I slept the dreams came too.

The dreams were oh so real to me

And God said that they will surely come true.

During my second trimester people started noticing my glow.

They started probing and asking questions

Am I pregnant? They want to know.

People came to me with heavy hearts,

Telling me of their woes.

I just lean over to them and say

Jesus already knows.

Visits to the Written Word are essential right now

Oh!! a Braxton-Hicks pain hit!

I bow down and say "Ow."

My last trimester, I am coming to the end.

Am I ready for the delivery?

Am I ready? It all depends…

I'm coming to a realization

That I'm about to deliver soon.

What more do I have to do?

Is the birth in May or will it be June?

Writing plain on paper

What is written in my heart,

I know God gave me gifts and talents

But I don't know where to start.

I'm starting to go into labor and its almost time to push.

Now nine centimeters more to wait before the birth of my purpose.

During my labor cycle its God's hand that I hold.

He cools me when I'm hot and warms me when I'm cold.

The pains are getting stronger they are hard to sustain.

Should I get an epidural or should I just endure the pain.

I wonder what I'm having I know it will be big.

It's too late to turn back now and it's too late to renege.

The pressure is getting great,

Tears are coming down my face.

My breathing I have to stagger

And I may even have to pace.

Okay the Head Physician says now it's time to PUSH

He says He sees the head.

The hair is just like a bush.

All that God put inside of me:

My life purpose will soon be revealed.

No matter how big your purpose is

Remember Jesus' blood seals the deal.

16. Can You Paint?　5/7/2009

Reds, blues, oranges, and yellows,

Can you paint a perfect picture?

Can you show in your painting your true colors?

You know, what is really going on with you?

Do not hide things or keep secrets

For whatever is hidden will come to light.

Share it with someone you trust so it can be prayed out.

In the name of Jesus.

Can you paint your thoughts?

What are you thinking?

Is it pleasant or is it death?

Look at it from another perspective.

For maybe it's something in you that needs

To die so that you may live for Christ.

Can you paint your life?

What is your life filled with?

Hopefully, it's filled with love, patience, and other fruits of the spirit;

And that you are working on that,

Which does not please God.

Here, here is an easel, assorted paints, crayons, and pencils…

What will you paint?

Remember, to Jesus you are a perfect picture.

For He died so that you would be made complete.

17. My Song (date unknown)

When I first started my song,

I had no idea what it would sound like.

I just stood stage fright

In front of the mic.

I stood there forgetting when to come in.

Before it began, I was hoping it would end.

Something inside me told me to get a grip.

Lifted up my hands and began to worship.

All of a sudden

A familiar beat started to resound.

Words started flowing

So much easier now.

I started to get

Into my element.

The song was beautiful.

It was God sent.

I started to understand

The rhythm of my life,

By listening to my heart

And hearing Christ.

It all became clear;

I came to know that song.

When I sing it,

I forget about things gone wrong.

Now I am the happiest that

I've ever been.

When tribulations come

I'll just start to sing

My song.

18. You Are the Music to My Song 1/2002

You are the music to my song,

The melody to my soul.

You've been the completion to my life

More than you'll ever know.

You are the music to my song;

You've always been there for me.

You've been my accompaniment through various times,

Always making me the BEST I can be.

When you play it is an

Epiphany of grace.

And when I hear the sound of music,

I see your beautiful F-A-C-E.

You are the music to my song,

We've been so close, but yet so far.

Working graciously together,

Playing each and every bar.

You are the music to my song,

I've always loved you so.

I have from the first time

That we'd ever performed at a show.

Whenever you stroke these

Black and white keys,

My heart is filled

With beautiful harmonies.

We've made beautiful music together,

We have throughout the years.

Sometimes we were so in sync,

That we've brought people to tears.

Because you are the music, and my life, the song.

This is written for a special friend.

19. Stop

Stop all these things before it's too late and your life at stake.

Stop your swearing.

Stop sleeping around.

Stop being so prideful.

Stop putting others down.

Stop your gossiping.

Stop talking back to your mother.

Stop being so angry.

Stop killing your brother.

For you, young ladies:

In order to receive love from another,

You must first love yourself.

If you don't, don't expect for someone else.

For you, young gents:

In order to succeed in life,

You must be the best that you can be.

If you don't, don't expect it to be easy.

It's not too late to change your ways, for there is life after death.

After you'd OD on drugs,

After you failed in school,

After you got an abortion,

After you've been abused,

AS long as you have breath, you can begin to live.

So, stop all these things before it's too late and your life at stake.

20. Jesus wants U

Wanted:

Strong people, to enlist in the army of God.

Talents a plus, but not necessary.

In Jesus' care,

He'll teach you who you are in Him.

Teach you how to run from sin,

Teach that with Him you'd always win,

Teach you to take up your weapon.

In Jesus' care,

He'll teach you the fruits of spirit,

Teach you how to obtain honor and merit,

Teach you that you are worth it.

Teach you the victory is yours, just you claim it.

21. Message to the Worship Leaders 7/3/2006

Open your mouth and worship our Father in spirit and in truth.

Worship is Warfare.

Battles are being won in the spiritual realm

The battles are not yours, anyway; it's the Lord's.

We have an awesome responsibility of ushering people into His presence,

Where they will find joy, peace and most of all love.

The notes that we sing are spiritual weapons.

Take up your weapon and stand post.

Each note that we sing is stabbing at the evil one and his boys.

When you are unsure of the note, ask the heavenly host to sing it for you then open your mouth.

The times that you are hurting and going through is the best time to sing praises unto Almighty God.

The result: restoration and reconciliation.

And that's when you sucker punch the devil.

Open your mouth and worship our Father in spirit and in truth.

Tell Him how much you love Him, and He will show you how much He loves you.

You will take refuge in the Lord's loving arms.

Jeremiah says He wants to prosper you and not to harm you.

By faith you will receive what God has promised you. So, Worship. Don't waver and don't get weary.

Praise His Holy Name.

Lift up your voice Zion so that God can be glorified.

Open your mouth and worship our Father in spirit and in truth.

We all know that the devil is defeated, so just open your mouth in Jesus' name.

Amen

22. Victim to Victor (Heart Surgery)

I was a victim and didn't know it.

I knew I was a daughter, sister, mother, author, psalmist, and a poet.

People telling you that you are no good

Or their actions showing you that you are not enough.

Up goes a wall of brick, stone or even wood,

And normalizing the pain because pain is too rough.

You praise God and read His Word every day.

Singing songs that you have the victory.

But that pain you have harbored deep, deep inside

God whispers in your ear, "You never gave that to me."

You thought you dealt with the pain, but circumstances made light of it.

It was brought to light in the form of disrespect.

Instead of dealing, you just retreat.

Instead of letting God in, you walk in the state of defeat.

Powers and principalities keep sending people and circumstances to keep you in victim mode,

Causing you to forget that Christ died on the cross to pay the debt you owed.

This causes you to react and not to respond.

Change is also painful but in a good way.

My eyes have been opened a new day has dawned.

I asked God to take out of me what was deep inside that is

not like HIM.

Just as I got new glasses, I can finally see.

What was deep inside eating at me.

Surgery is taking place to take out the decay that has been living inside of me.

Just like when a bad tooth has to come out of your mouth,

This is one of the reasons why relationships had gone south.

People will try to put you back to pre-surgery.

But walk in confidence because that is just trick of the enemy.

It will take time to learn your new self.

Discard all the old stuff, clean out all your closets and all shelves.

Fear, guilt, low self-esteem, and shame, please show them to the door.

In its place fill it with love.

I am a victor: a victim, no more.

P.S. Have post-surgery appointment to make sure your sutures are healing nicely.

Keep the area clean, free of fear, guilt, low self-esteem, and shame.

Keeping healthy is a daily battle and is not easy.

Don't take it lightly.

Guard your hearts and minds and love, for it conquers all.

Oh

And make sure you say sorry to all the people that you unconsciously steamed rolled over along the way.

23. These are the Last Days (date unknown)

These are the last days.

You know that because it is written,

Death is upon us no matter the age.

From being shot to the cancer stage

An outrage!

From the Boston bombings to the changing marriage craze,

And people collecting benefits from the grave.

The Bible says it will rain on the just and the unjust,

On people who pray, to people who cuss.

Don't be surprised if trouble comes; it is a must

While we are going through problems, in God we must trust.

Darkness will come.

All craziness will break loose under the sun.

People will sin and think they are having fun.

Sins like adultery lust and fornication,

Preaching blasphemy on every occasion,

Confusion!

Fulfill the greatest commandment, which is to love one another,

Encourage and fellowship with each other,

Pray to cover.

Read the Bible, discover.

For long life, honor your father and mother.

Be a Jesus lover.

Hold on to Jesus,

He is solid ground.

Before HIM you are lost, now are found.

Under HIS covering you will be safe and sound.

Profound.

Give Jesus worship and praise,

And don't get caught up in the worldly maze,

Where people are collecting benefits from the grave.

From the Boston bombings to the changing marriage craze,

Where death is upon us no matter the age.

From being shot to the cancer stage,

An outrage!

These are the signs that these are the last days.

24. Rushing 4-3-00

Look at you, rushing,

Running here and there.

Getting this, getting that,

Trying to make it there.

Rushing, Rushing, Rushing

You shoulda woke up an hour ago.

Oh no, what time is it?

You don't even know.

You missed the bus, a car crashed,

Traffic back up down the street.

Cars beeping their horns, trying to rush, they
have the time to beat.

Rushing, Rushing, Rushing

Trying to make it thru the day.

Just make sure you make time to rest,

After you spent your whole entire day,

Rushing….

25. You Win

There's shooting from the foul line,
Don't wanna run out of time.
Shoot the two and do it again
You're gonna win.

Get with the rhythm of the game.
The other team will do the same.
Three pointers you are trying to get,
Shuffle, hop, step, net.
Opposition is in your face,
Trying to figure out your pace.
The other team is up by one.
One of them hits your arm.

There's shooting from foul line
Don't wanna run out of time

Shoot the two and You got both in

You win!!!